THE
Haunted
Forest
Trilogy

THE
Haunted Forest Trilogy

Poetry by
Jarod K. Anderson

Boyle
&
Dalton

Book Design & Production:
Boyle & Dalton
www.BoyleandDalton.com

Hardback ISBN: 978-1-63337-817-9

Volume One: Field Guide to the Haunted Forest
Originally published by Crooked Wall Press
Copyright © 2020 Jarod K. Anderson
ISBN: 9798572931358
Publishing Note:
"Solar Power" originally appeared as "Planters' Season" in Star*Line, Fall 2016
"Almost Certainly a Time Traveler" originally appeared in Asimov's, March/April 2017

Volume Two: Love Notes from the Hollow Tree
Originally published by Crooked Wall Press
Copyright © 2022 Jarod K. Anderson
ISBN: 9798826128046

Volume Three: Leaf Litter
Originally Published by Crooked Wall Press
Copyright © 2023 Jarod K. Anderson
ISBN: 9798870221885
Publishing Note:
"Whale Fall," "Afterlife," and "City" originally appeared in Atmos (Nov 2023)
"Around the Corners" originally appeared in Nightmare Magazine (Aug 2022)

Printed in the United States of America
1 3 5 7 9 10 8 6 4 2

For Leslie and Arthur.

For Molly and Dave.

For the woods.

For the readers and supporters who remind me why writing matters.

Contents

Author's Note

THERE'S A BIT OF MYSTERY baked into the word "trilogy" as it applies to these three poetry collections.

I am certainly not finished writing poetry, so why group these books?

At first, it was an impulse without an explanation.

I felt these three books were connected before I could articulate exactly why.

In a personal sense, these collections represent a shift in my creative life, a new season of my writing. In the years before publishing *Field Guide to the Haunted Forest*, I had taken a long break from poetry and the poems in that collection (and the two that followed) were the stepping stones that led me back to the form.

They also led me away from old ideas about what poetry was, its purpose and strictures. I learned to take myself less seriously by taking connection and communication more seriously.

I learned that I didn't want to lecture. I wanted to have a chat, ideally while walking a woodland path.

Yet, this trilogy is not simply in conversation with my past, it is also in conversation with itself. I felt a narrative thread running through this haunted forest like a muttering creek. That narrative echoed my own ever-evolving relationship with nature.

At first, I wanted to be "correct," I wanted fact and terminology on my side. I wanted a *Field Guide to the Haunted Forest*, the landscape I discovered without and within, concealing nascent meaning and messages like phantoms drifting between the boughs.

Next, I began to shift from objective to subjective modes of appreciation. The woods were not simply a collection of things to know. There was personal meaning to discover beneath the trees, meaning aimed at me specifically. I discovered *Love Notes from the Hollow Tree*, a more personal kind of connection between tangible nature and the more abstract meaning taking root within my own perception.

Lastly, I wanted to honor the cyclical, seasonal nature I began to understand as the underpinnings of all fruitful growth and development. There are conspicuous examples of spring blossoms in nature and in our own lives, but there is also *Leaf Litter*, a kind of aftermath that is itself a beautiful, worthy part of the cycle of growth and renewal. Within my own love of nature and through the mental health struggles that color so much of my creative life, I began to make peace with the idea that steady, linear growth was not the ideal I once thought it was.

These three collections represent a cycle I often observe in my own process of understanding. It's an interest in fact, shifting to a focus on subjective interpretation and meaning-making, culminating in a broad acceptance that growth often relies on seasons of dormancy and renewal. This reflects the nature I cherish, without and within. It also reflects the shape of *The Haunted Forest Trilogy*.

Jarod K. Anderson
Delaware, Ohio
June, 2024

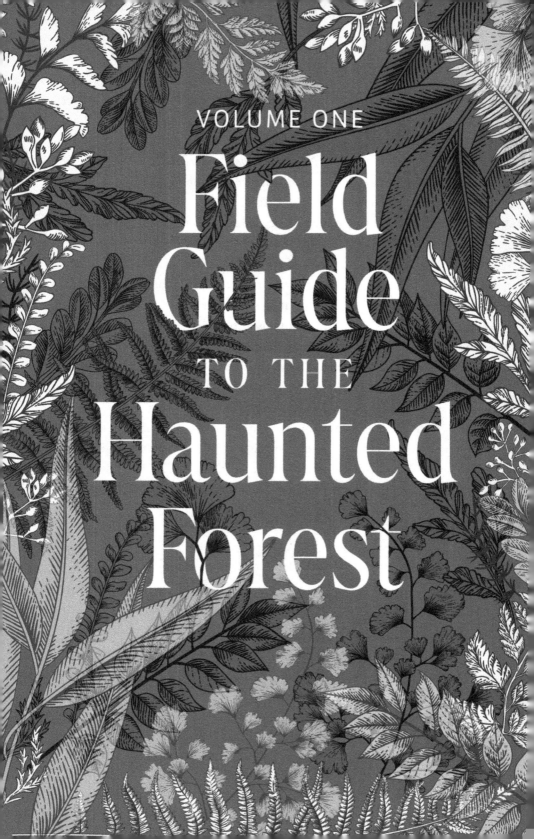

VOLUME ONE

Field Guide

TO THE

Haunted

Forest

Author's Note

POETRY IS AN ODD CREATURE. Some of the work in this collection feels like poetry to me, the poetry I grew up writing and studying. Some of it feels more like a cousin to poetry. Yet, I believe all the text in this collection belongs here. This book focuses on the ideas and themes that matter to me. Gratitude to nature. Magic hiding in plain sight. The beauty of impermanence and our close kinship with the world we inhabit. Many of these poems started as social media posts or fragments of scripts for The CryptoNaturalist, my fiction podcast about strange nature and a man who finds beauty and meaning in the unusual. I hope the ideas in this book are useful to you. They have been very useful to me.

Jarod K. Anderson
Delaware, Ohio
November, 2020

Technically Speaking

You can look at any human life
as the sum of a complex collection of chemical reactions,

in much the same way as you can look at any beautiful painting
as a simple collection of pigments,

Which is to say,
you can miss the point of anything.

Lump

A lump of iron formed in the heart of a red super-giant.
So long ago.
So far from here.
There was a silent explosion.
There was a trip across lightyears, cold and hard,
drifting like a dandelion seed through a dark forever.
The lump came to Earth.
It was forged into a sword.
A hammer.
A ring.
It flowed red through the blood of a leaping deer,
but it was still the star. The long, dark journey.
Crimson in the veins of a sleeping child,
but still the silent explosion.
And it brought what it was
wherever it traveled.

Sit With Me

I'm not trying to write a tailored suit.
I'm trying to write boot socks, warm from the dryer.
There's an endless autumn in me,
scenting my thoughts like campfire smoke.
I write for the weather I know.

Woodland You

It's easy to look at the contours of a forest and feel
a bone deep love for nature.
It's less easy to remember that the contours of your own body
represent the exact same nature.
The pathways of your mind.
Your dreams,
dark and strange as sprouts curling beneath a flat rock.
Your regret,
bitter as the citrus rot of old cut grass.
It's the same as the nature you make time to love.
That you practice loving.
The forest. The meadow. The sweeping arm of a galaxy.
You are as natural as any postcard landscape
and deserve the same love.

Home Safety Tip

If you are awoken by a strange sound,
make a stranger sound.

If there's no response,
congratulations.

You are the monster now.

Get out of bed.
You don't need to sleep anymore.

Now, all you need are the shadows
and the endless whispers of dark corners.

Naming the River

The water in your body is just visiting.
It was a thunderstorm a week ago.
It will be an ocean soon enough.
Most of your cells come and go like morning dew.
We are more weather pattern than stone monument.
Sunlight on mist. Summer lightning.
Your choices outweigh your substance.

The Chain

You were once very much part of your mother's body.

The same is true for your mother and her mother
and so on back to the beginning.
It's a biological chain that stretches back to the first living cell
awakening in a young ocean
millions of years before the first spoken name.

We are links in that chain.
Can you feel its weight?
A clear path back to ancient waters.

You are here. In modernity. As familiar as thirst.
Just remember what else you are.
Your mother. Her mother. The ancient seas beneath a thin, new sky.

Host

To invading germs, you are a jungle
full of hungry tigers.

To your gut bacteria, you are a warm orchard
of perpetual bounty.

To your eyelash mites, you are a walking fortress
and a mountaintop pasture.

How many generations have you hosted?
What do they name the wilderness of you?

The Wood

When you were born, your enthusiasm was a red flame atop a mountain of fuel. As you age, the fuel burns low. No one warns you. Yet, with intention, you can learn to feed that warming fire long after the fuel you were born with is ash on the wind. Be kind to yourself. Learn this.

They say cut all the wood you think you will need for the night, then double it. Cut it during the daylight when fuel seems irrelevant. Dead limbs hanging low, sun-dried, hungry for fire. The night can be longer than we expect. The wind can be colder than we predict. The dark beneath the trees is absolute. Gather the fuel. Double it.

Family Resemblance

Our blood is red because of the iron we inherited from the Earth.
Iron to bind the oxygen from trees and phytoplankton.
Our blood and breath are hand-me-downs.
The landscape is not scenery.
It's family. Notice the resemblance.

Our blood is mostly water.
Iron to bind oxygen, built using the energy of sunlight.
Water. Earth. Air. Fire.
You may feel separated from the natural world,
but just look at what you are.
Look at how you live.
You are not born to this place. You are born of this place.

Take one square meter of your bedroom,
of the deepest abyss of sunless sea,
of the brutal emptiness of interstellar space.
Put them side by side and see the harmony.
They are all children of the same natural laws.

Our bodies speak of contradiction.
Bones and soft tissue. Teeth and lips. Sensitive resilience.
What strong family resemblance we share
with the landscapes that shaped us.
Wind and stone. Rivers and oaks.
This old dance of opposing forces
creating a unified whole.

Unscripted

We all consume so many purposefully crafted stories
that it's easy to forget life doesn't follow
conventional narrative structure.
We can't wait for our climax.
We don't have character arcs.
We live and then we don't.
There is no culmination in success or failure.
We are not curated collections of achievements or mishaps.
Don't fear you won't be good enough.
Just be here.
Present in this dance between joy and sorrow.
The plot is happening now.
Today is the story of you and me.

The Treatment

I can't say spending time in nature heals depression.
For me, the outdoors changes sadness from a pain
to be endured to a state to be experienced.
It's still sadness.
But in the context of green growing things
under a limitless sky, sadness is simplified.
Not a wound. A tile in the mosaic.

Even so, depression needs more.

I resisted trying therapy for a long time
because I thought I was too smart for it.
Here's the thing.
You can't think your way out of depression
any more than you can think your way out of drowning.
Asking for a life-jacket is more important
than knowing the physics of buoyancy.

The Text

You are a unique sentence built from the alphabet of our universe.
The letters were here before you and the story will march on
long after you've been read,
but you will forever be a part of the definitive text of existence.
It's too late for you not to matter.

Plain as Day

Your eye is a collection of cells
that evolved to borrow radiation
from a fiery ball of superheated hydrogen and helium
in order to gather information
about objects outside your physical reach.

Vision is a kind of divination
shaped and fueled by a cosmic inferno.
This can't be true.

It very much is.

Identity

There's a silver bell in your rib cage.
When you're trying to fall asleep, you feel for it,
like a tongue mapping a chipped tooth.

One day,
you'll find it and it will ring cold and clear as an autumn lake.
That sound will be who you are,
warm certainty like a belly full of hot soup,
until it fades.

Then, you'll search again.

Sentry

Kindness. Gentleness. Empathy.

These things are fires shining in the forest night.
They must be tended,
but in tending them we are illuminated.

We become a target for things that thrive in darkness.

So, as ever, love is risk.
And, as ever,
worth the danger.

The Whole

All living things are the same living thing,
a branching tree spreading from a shared past.

This unified creature grows in four dimensions,
and the illusion of separation we see here
on the budding branch-tips
appears because we can't view time
the way we see our own vital hands.

It's as real as the moment mitochondria moved in to stay.
And maybe, in the end, we'll feel it like warm coffee on the tongue,
like skin against skin.

I wish I could wander back through my ancestors
like a steppingstone path.

To Ireland. To Africa.
Past organisms that were never named by humans.
To the sunlit waters where life began to feel its own strange power.
To the forest of hands that lifted me up into my own simple life.

I wish I could know the whole,
so I could love it more completely.

Candle Facts #1

If you whisper a secret to a candle flame,
then all fire everywhere will know that secret.

The words will crackle in every campfire
and churn like an ocean deep in the belly of the Earth.

Fire will translate your words to smoke and ash,
telling no one but the sky.

Together in Absurdity

The entirety of your personality resides in an organ the size of a guinea pig encased in the living stone of your skull.

Your thoughts are spun like cotton candy from flesh and electricity and you expect to be perfect?

All the billions of humans on Earth are living
this same strange, awkward truth.
There's a reason we have empathy.
We need it.

The Big Bang

The universe is an ongoing explosion.

That's where you live.

In an explosion.

Of course, we absolutely don't know what living is.
We don't know what happens in the gulf
between molecules and cells.

Sometimes, atoms arranged in a certain way just get very, very haunt-
ed.

That's us.

When an explosion explodes hard enough,
dust wakes up and thinks about itself.

And then writes about it.

Many Hands

The world will always be troubled.
This is true.

You deserve to feel happy and comfortable.
This is also true.

If you feel the first truth undermines the second, I offer this:

Own a share of the virtuous work toward solutions.
Don't burden your worth with global outcomes.

The good and the evil are happening concurrently.
The choice to focus on the good is itself
a way to defy the evil.

Reaction

The first living cell on Earth was a spark.
It ignited a chain reaction that thundered across millions of years,
an evolving blaze of lives and needs and firsts and lasts.

The whole of that raging fire of history and happenstance
burns inside you right now.
You are that continuity of matter and motion.

Your irrational fear of centipedes.
An old scar like a barbed hook.
The effortless bravery of your kindness.

You are the flame racing down the fuse.

Thoughts Like Ivy

Your brain,
the seat of your consciousness,
is as natural as a leaf.

It arose in the world in the same way as a finch's wing.
A cricket's song.

Wherever you are right now,
the part of you that's awake and reading this
is in nature.

There's a temptation to think of ourselves as separate
here in the warm quarters of civilization.
But our thoughts?

Our thoughts echo from an ancient wilderness.

Potential

You can be still while the world is whirling.
You can be silent while your heart is thundering.
You can be alone while your memory is teeming.

You can live forever in the span of a moment.
You can grow kindness in the soil of hatred.
You can decide purpose. You can decide victory.

Vulnerable

You are not safe.
Your birth was reckless.
Lightning strikes without reason.
Countless simple mishaps may be fatal.
To live is to collect risk like a bee collects nectar.

Yet there is hope in fragility.

Our goal was never safety.
Our success is not measured in forever.
Our years are seasoning, but the meal is meaning.
Our task is to become our truest selves and to smile
at the knowledge that we will not succeed.

Limits

You won't see most of this planet.
Under each rock.
Beneath the water.
Secrets of air and soil.

Can you feel the joy behind this limitation?
That there is always a new thing to discover,
a new way to grow,
is one of the sweetest parts of living,

and it's free and inexhaustible.

Every Life is a Sound

The soft susurrus of jellyfish who have never known the shore.
The sharp sizzle of deer fleeing through autumn corn.

These sounds belong to the same unfinished poem as you
and your fistful of years like copper coins.

It wouldn't be poetry without you.

The Impossible

Bats can hear shapes.
Plants can eat light.
Bees can dance maps.

We can hold all these ideas at once and feel
both heavy and weightless
with the absurd beauty of it all.

Unwritten

50,000 years ago,
an elk was struck by lightning and lived.

The ache of it stayed in her bones the rest of her life.
There was no human there to see it or record it in words,

yet it's just as much a part of earth's essential history as any song
lingering in a billion human minds.

Calibration

Weigh a leaf in your palm.
Imperceptible.
A green whisper.
A cool nothing.
Weigh it again in your lungs,
with the iron in your blood.
Feel your genes clinging to those soft green cells like ivy on an oak.
Weigh the leaf once more with your love.
Trust this measure most.

Blueprint

If you write out the basic facts of trees,
but framed as technology,
it sounds like impossible sci-fi nonsense.

Self-replicating, solar-powered machines
that synthesize carbon dioxide and rainwater
into oxygen and sturdy building materials
on a planetary scale.

What do we make that compares?

Fossil

The fossil is not the animal.

The fossil is not the bones of the animal.

The fossil is the stone's memory of the bones of the animal.

And that's a poetry older than words.

Candle Facts #2

A lit candle is a tiny, flickering animal
standing on top of all the food it will eat in its lifetime.

A candle is a leash.

They let us tame an ancient, devouring force of nature,
older than life,
and stick it in a little jar on the shelf.

A candle is a pet god.

Thanks to Birds

Birds are dinosaurs who shrugged off a couple apocalypses.
Some eat bone marrow.
Some drink nectar.
They outswim fish in the sea.
They smile politely at gravity's demands.
I am grateful to see them. I am grateful to feed them.
I am grateful to know them.

Losing

Our muscles are prompted to grow by failure,
healing from countless micro-injuries.

Our minds, science, and technology
are similarly nourished by defeat.

We are creatures born to thrive
on the borderlands of ruin.

Home is a valley between saw-toothed peaks of loss.
Here we sow failure and harvest miracles.

Seriously Though

If you can make peace with the unlikely fact
that squids the size of school buses patrol the dark oceans
at a depth that would crush you to paste,

then I have faith you can also make peace with the unlikely fact
that you are worthy of all the happiness you have imagined.

Orcas

Somewhere, there are orcas.

I'm in my little gray house in Ohio
surrounded by the stale air of winter indoors,

but somewhere there are orcas.

It's an easy fact to forget.
It's easy to shrink your world to what you can see.

But thankfully, somewhere, there are orcas.

Sometimes, my world is all sun-faded plastic
scrawled along the roadside in a scribble of petty meanness,

but somewhere there are orcas.

We all know facts that are as inert as chalk dust,
but some knowledge is medicine.

Flawless

Things that are perfect
are dead things.

Empty things.

A silence beyond change or challenge.
An endpoint.
A blank page.

You are a wonderfully messy thing.

An impossible thing made of salt
and rainwater.
Meat and electricity.

A dream with teeth.

You're too good for perfection.

Crush

Today you did things that humans 50 years ago wouldn't believe
and 200 years ago would struggle to imagine.

You know the names of planets
and the shapes of the bones inside you.

You comprehend death and make art.
You are a surpassingly strange animal, worthy of study.

I love you.

The Truth About Owls

You flinch at leaf shadows
tumbling across your driveway
and the shadows notice you flinching.

The thought gets under their skin,
starts them asking questions to your back
as you walk away.

"Are we something to fear?"

Two nights later,
the shadows pile into three dimensions,
hop twice, and fly off on soundless wings.

Economics

We borrow our atoms.
The universe owns them.

The universe borrows our love and wonder.
Those belong to us.

Nameless

Remember this:
Someone made-up the word "sky."

Likewise the word "wolf."
The words "leaf" and "raindrop."

Words are jewels.

Precious to us, but small and finite.

Forget these words and try to name these things anew.
You will feel their scope and meaning weigh upon your mind.

Pour a new word into the sky and see it fade like smoke.

Look for the noise that equals the reality of wolves.

How will you wrap such things up in syllables
And set them upon your tongue.

Soft

Our fingers are built more for feeling than fighting.
Nerve endings prioritized over talons or claws.

Our relatively modest strength.
Our long, vulnerable road to adulthood.

Our species' success is the story of betting
on understanding over brutality.

It's the wise, patient bet.

Psst

The universe is an event, not a place.
Don't seek to own.
Witness.

Entangled

The problem with history is that it's full of spiders.
They scribbled webs over the invention of doorways
and crawled into the bellies of our sleeping orators.

Show me the liar saint that never killed or cursed one.
And when we load the beds and dark corners into ships
like silver needles tugging our thin threads through space

we might declare a hasty victory over recluse and funnel-web.
But, they'll be there. Strung up just at face-level
in the dark paths between the rocks and suns.

Pact

Iron in birds' inner ears
helps them navigate using the Earth's magnetic field.

In other words,
the birds carry within them a piece of the Earth,

a talisman, which speaks to the Earth and whispers
its knowledge back to the birds.

Hey.

Your matter recalls cosmic explosions
and you tasted oblivion before you learned your own name.

Fear nothing.

Home

An ant crosses your carpet.
A spider weaves a pattern older than mammals beneath your stairs.

Just nod,
breathe,
and think,

good.
It's all still here.
The forest, the mountains, the desert.

At home in my home.

The sterile white box is the stranger.
Not the ant.
Not the spider.

Truth and Fact

"Love is just chemicals."

Yeah?

So is the churning inferno of the sun.
So is the bedrock of the earth.
So is the living fountain of a blooming cherry tree.

If you need to call upon the word "magic"
to fully appreciate the beauty of all that which is vivid and real,

do so.

Truth and fact are sisters, not twins.

Statecraft

Night is Earth's shadow.
Your shadow is a tiny, you-shaped night.

Your night and Earth's night know each other.

They have conversations that you can't hear and wouldn't understand
anyway.

Don't begrudge them this.

Your shadow is an embassy for the nation of you.
It's wise to foster diplomacy
with a neighbor older than starlight.

Worthless

One dangerous illusion of modernity is the link
between cost and value.

Could we afford the true cost of rain?

Can we calculate a price for the work of phytoplankton
producing the oxygen we need?

Our survival will require us to understand value independent of cost.

Relativity

There.
Now.
A sharp stone juts from an icy sea.
crowded with gulls screaming accusations at a flinty sky,

the wind hides daggers and beneath the waves
something rich in teeth swims lazy circles.

Here.
Now.
I hope this truth makes your current surroundings seem
more warm and welcoming.

Owl

The best poems are owls.
A reflection of the landscape,
but singular and strange,

smooth and effortless as smoke.
A trick of the eye that scatters bones in the underbrush,
hard and real.

This and More

The world is the sound of tree shapes
decoded in a bat's brain.
The world is electric fields
flexing in the mind of a shark.
The world is a landscape of scents,
recalled by a wolf like an old friend.
The world is a mosaic of temperature shifts
on the tip of a python's snout.
The world is you
making meaning
from marks on this page.

Your Maker

The sun isn't alive.
It's better than alive.

It swims,
self-sustaining,
through endless void.

All we in its orbit think and do
is a byproduct
of its audacious existence.

Waiting Up

Autumn is a kind of nightfall.
Plants and animals withdraw into sleep,
curling inward around the warm spark of their lives,

waiting for the spring dawn.

We who stay awake
are witnesses to the dormant, secret times.
Seasonally nocturnal.

We keep watch through the cold and dark.

Ownership

Fish flashed in mountain streams long before the first human.
Honey was sweet and falling snow was graceful
before a person noticed such things.
This world is not here for us.
We are simply fortunate to live here.

Almost Certainly a Time Traveler

I think my bones remember, even if I don't.
My teeth feel like time-traveler's teeth.
Temporality skitters along my femur
Like centipedes on a fallen branch.

I know how to do it.
When I concentrate on the idea,
Schematics bloom inside my skull,
Vivid diagrams pulsing with déjà vu.

It would take all I own and more,
An absolute and final turning away
From the people I love. From simple comforts.
A gamble aimed at erasing its own necessity.

I'm no daredevil with causality. No crusader.
Erasing the old atrocities would kill our present
And cowardly and selfish as I am
I wouldn't do it for lottery winnings.

I know I wouldn't because I haven't.

But I can imagine reasons
And I ache with the feeling that my life,
As familiar and yielding as an old paperback,
Means that the mission was accomplished.

I am desperately thankful for my own fingers
As if I gave reality a fat lip just to keep them
And each word my wife speaks, love or shopping lists,
Is worth innovation bordering on absurdity.

I can almost remember doing it.

On evenings after work, I take inventory of my life.
I do it for the version of me that made the leap
And if I was bold and brilliant and risked all,

Then, as I watch sitcom reruns in bed,
Safe and whole with my wife softly snoring,
I know I have been well rewarded for my efforts.
I owe it to myself to notice.

Spoiler Alert

I just read ahead to the last page of your life and it turns out that you were always worthy of love and hope and surpassing kindness.

Dying Practice

Every memory is a ghost and the house they haunt is you.

27-year-old me is gone from the world,
but echoes of him remain.

The same is true for 17-year-old me
and 7-year-old me.

Those people no longer exist.

But I hear their footsteps in the attic,

walking where I can't
where I will join them
in the memory of a future me.

Solar Power

When the winds talked back,
there was an ember on the tongue of the world.
Each word glowed red as fresh-dug clay.

We didn't know the words,
so we pressed our ears to conch shells
and listened to the roar of our own veins.

Some blood rumbled shame
like the wordless chug of an engine
and others said, "all is well and always will be."

Our blood said to plant.

Seeds like sleek white birds
that smelled of ozone before a storm
and would spin on your open palm
forever.

They were not fast-growing crops
and the fields seemed fallow
under sunsets that rusted
trust and expectation,

but the day came.

At first, they looked like foxgloves
with fresh shoots spun from liquid glass
blooming chrome and circuitry.

They climbed hundreds of feet
and when they met the wind,
they greeted it in its own language,
syllables old as oceans.

The fruit we harvested
took our thirst and our hunger
and sizzled on our lips like rain on pavement.

When the winds talked back,
there was an ember on the tongue of the world
and we turned toward the heat like flowers toward the sun.

Lifespan

A firefly lives two months.
There are bristlecone pines standing today that have lived 5,000 years.

The vital dignity of each of these species is not measured in time.
Both are perfection.

Treat your time likewise.
Your moments deserve the same careful attention as your years.

In the End

You were a part of the sky on loan to a body.

A part of the sea that awoke to thought.

A part of the Earth who borrowed a name.

The essential piece of you that lingers is the love and knowledge that you set in motion while you moved through the waking world.

You are nature and nature will go on,

but there is kindness that only you can choose to bring to the world.

Our Craft

People make meaning like bees make honey.

Gathering experiences and images,
synthesizing them into something new,
rich,
uniquely ours.

Respect the meaning you make,
the family you choose,
the wisdom you craft,

sweet and golden on your tongue.

Mercy

The old you buzzes around your skull like a bee
in the kitchen window.
Don't swat it.
Be kind.

We must hope that our current selves will one day step aside to make
room for better versions of us.
Shuttle the old you outside in a mason jar.
Let it climb onto the lilac in the sun.

A Time for Choice

You are the mountain, but awake.
You are the rain, but breathing.
You are the forest, but unanchored.
You are the soil, but with choice.
You are the sunlight, but dreaming.

Soon, you will be these things again. Mountain. Rain. Forest. Sunlight.

So, what will you do until then?

Endpoint

One day,
your story will end
and all the choices you made will be frozen
like an insect in the amber of history.

Friend, this isn't meant to be grim.
Just a reminder that you are building something that will one day be
whole and complete.
So, build with purpose.

Better to be Safe

When he thinks of it,
my father tries to talk over the rain
like his voice is a place of its own
where we won't see my mother
closing her eyes each time we pass
the great grey smudge of a semi.

When we have a quiet moment,
in the safe places, she says the trucks
make her think of tasting her own blood,
like a penny on her tongue with one
cheek on the wet pavement
that should be cold, but isn't.

She tells me how the sky looks green
just before the tornado comes
and plucks the roof out into nothing
like the way black ice makes the breaks
useless, makes the steering wheel useless
makes joints, tendons, muscles useless.

When they found her cancer,
she shaved her own head, standing
at the kitchen counter while my father
canceled their cruise ship reservations.
She waited for weeks to tell my brother
and me. She said I was too busy
for an extra worry.

Unlearning Death

When we die, they may bury us or collect our ashes, but remember this: from baby teeth to skin cells and everything in between, most of the matter that has worn your name is already spread throughout the world. We bury our remains in the soil of our lifetimes.

Can you feel it? So many of the cells that have formed the community of your body have returned to nature. Most of the water that has fueled your life has returned to the sea. The substance of your form is not fixed. It flows like a river to and from the wilderness.

Moss doesn't think about being alive and mountains don't consider themselves to be dead. Death has no place in the vocabulary of nature. To worry about death is to forget that we, the moss, and the mountains are all part of an undiminished whole that isn't measured in breaths.

Holy

Let nature be your church.

Let the trees be your temple.

Let each nourishing breath be your sacred vow.

Let the shared spark of life be your holy order and,
if there is one prayer you can whisper into the ear of the world,

let it be "thank you."

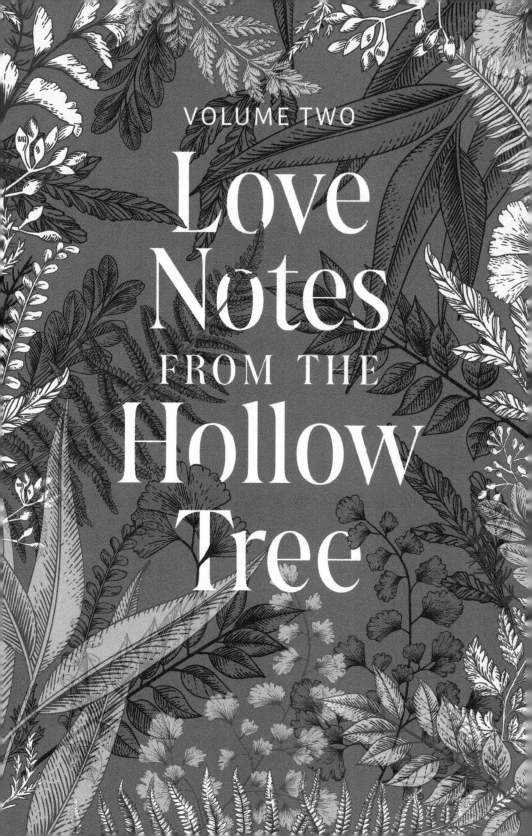

VOLUME TWO

Love
Notes
FROM THE
Hollow
Tree

Author's Note

THANK YOU FOR BEING HERE.

This is my second collection of poetry. My first collection *Field Guide to the Haunted Forest* sparked an amazing outpouring of love and support that enriched my life in myriad ways. I am sincerely grateful. In the introduction to my first collection, I said that much of the contents therein strayed from what I would traditionally call poetry. That remains true in these pages. I include scraps of prose and the germ of larger thoughts. I include bits of daydreams and outright silliness. I counted at least two dad jokes.

I have shaken the urge to apologize for the unusual nature of these collections.

I have eclectic interests, a stormy mind, and a need to write plainly and honestly.

I think the form of these collections is honest.

The structure of these books reflects my ADHD coupled with the highs and lows of my lifelong struggles with chronic depression. Perhaps most of all, these collections reflect my stubborn efforts to stay positive and celebrate kindness, both the willful kindness of people and the intrinsic kindness of nature.

All I can promise is that the words and ideas in this book felt worthy to me.

I hope you find them to be worthy too.

Jarod K. Anderson
Delaware, Ohio
April, 2022

Welcome

Step inside my cabin and hang your coat by the door.
You smell of snowfall and hemlock boughs.
I just fed the stove and the logs are whispering like radio static.
Soon, that white lace on your boots will pool on the floorboards,
making them shine like polished stone.
Rest here as long as you like.
It's no trouble that our meeting place is imaginary.
Many worthwhile things are.

Sting

To feel both utter frustration
and unqualified love for the world is the tension I'm learning to endure.

That feeling is the constant, crackling fire within my skull
and I am forever shutting my eyes against its stinging smoke,

while reaching toward its warm glow.

Cauldron

One day,
your skull will be as empty as a conch shell on a fence post,
full of wind and gentle quiet.

Today,
it's a cauldron of ghosts.
Flesh and electricity.
Water and memory.
A machine that makes reality.

Now.
Here.
Your skull is the garden where fact flowers
into meaning.

Bright

If I can hand you, a stranger, a bundle of words
like warm bread wrapped in cloth,
then this world can't be all bad.

Shelter

Often, my mental health does not cooperate with my creative goals.

Often, "does not cooperate" is an understatement.

I frame this as "brain weather."

Sudden snow may disrupt my gardening plans,
but the snow is not being malicious.

It's not my enemy.
It's just the weather.

During my decades of storms,
I have found that I can strengthen my shelters
and sharpen my forecasts,
but I still don't steer the clouds.

I find this metaphor helpful.

Natural hardships aren't punishments.
Nor do we own them.

So, we should not blame ourselves for our struggles
to stay warm and dry.

Zoom #1

Thanks for joining this Zoom call.

I know it's a Friday afternoon,
so I'll try to be brief.

A couple things about me.

I think the best things come in "clumps."

My skin is the stretched pink sky of a dawnless inner bog
full of hooting owls and hungry mud.

I wish to sleep for another 1,000 years,
but, deadlines, amiright?

How Much?

Your favorite song does not use all notes simultaneously.
Your favorite art is not all shades and hues.
The sweetness in life is as much a question of omission as inclusion.
Remember this when considering your own limitations.
The answer to "what is enough?" is not "all of it."

Getting Dressed

Today,
you may be as natural as a new leaf unfolding in silent softness above
a river valley.

Tomorrow,
you may be as natural as the crushing deep of the ocean floor,
where darkness is a clenched fist.

Choose the nature you need for the day you face.
Wear it well.

Cartographer

When we are born,
we arrive on the shores of a wilderness —
our minds.

We search for shelter.
We tumble into ravines.
We taste the berries that nourish and the ones that leave us
delirious in the mud.

All our lives we struggle to find footing in the forests of ourselves.
There are strange hills inside our thoughts.
Slowly, through messy effort, we become
native to these inner landscapes.

Don't be ashamed
of your stumbles, your scars, your sleepless nights.
You are here.
Wild and whole.

Learning to map the clouds.

Open Secret

Everyone has a story.
With a castle.
And a lady in white.
And children who smile at the space over your shoulder.
And the old stone well.
And a clockface on the moon.
And blue lights above the swamp.
And the smell of cellar soil in her hair.
Everyone has that same story.
We're just too polite to discuss it.

When All Else Fails

I have to assume that in the fullness of time,
at least once,
a mouse has used a mushroom as an umbrella.

I think, today,
that's enough to keep me going.

Could Be

There is so much that might exist,
but doesn't.

I feel the gulf between words and meaning,
so vast it empties me to consider.

There.
Now.

The universe has shifted and there's a moth wing at its center,
gray as ash.

Now again.

A dandelion seed tumbling skyward.

And we all tumble with it.

An Emerald Heaven

I hope there is life elsewhere in the universe.

I don't care about aliens and advanced technology.
I just want one planet that is all moss.
A perfect sphere of soft, green carpet.

I hope it exists and that no human foot ever dents its plush,
perfect surface.

Book of Earth

Stone writes the best eulogies.

Seashells pressed like flowers between pages of shale.
The poetry of petrification.

That T-Rex skull hasn't been bone for millions of years,
But it's here.

Memory without language.
Art without intent.

It's all still here.

Pub

As a young American with Irish ancestry,
my romanticized Ireland was a place where even in dive bars they love
poetry.

Sticky floors and Seamus Heaney.

I've never been to Ireland.

And I've come to distrust white America's talk of ancestry,
but the internet is certainly a dive bar

and there's enough poetry carved into the back booths
to keep me romantic.

Epitaph

Our bodies have died many times.

These aren't the cells you were born with.
A new skin each month.
Neuroplasticity building the plane mid-flight.

We in the pilot's chairs are already ghosts.
Here and not here.
Built of memories the way a beach is built of sand.

Shifting.
Ships anchored to fog.

To live is to haunt.

Kin

If you've ever grabbed a stick
from the ground and thought "oh, this is a good stick,"
then we're family.

The Ache

When we feel pained or drained by the ugliness in the world,
it is because we are mourning.
We mourn for our love of what the world could be,
for a place that isn't here, but should be.

That pain is the overwhelming goodness in you hungering for an echo
of itself.
What is. What was. What could be.

It is a terrible mark of honor to mourn.
It means we have the courage to love
in an imperfect, impermanent world.

It means we sided with difficult tenderness
over numbing indifference.

An Honest Appraisal

You are good enough and your worth isn't dependent on your
achievements.

It's not just an affirmation.
It's true.

It seems like your worth is based on your achievements
in much the same way it seems like the sun is made of fire.

Both are common sense.
Both are incorrect.

Common sense is common because at first glance it appears true,
not because it actually is.

We build complex lives,
but if you're feeling lost or trapped,
look to your foundations and make sure this basic truth
is there in the stone.

You are good enough and your worth isn't dependent on your
achievements.

What achievements could two-year-old-you claim?
Were you worthless then?
So, what has changed?

Expectation?
Whose expectations?

Let's say achievements are partly built from your worth.

Okay.

They are also part luck, and context, and timing, and happenstance, and privilege, and opportunity,
and the subjective priorities of the people defining "achievement" for this year/place/culture/community.

Be proud of your achievements.
But understand that they are not your worth.
They are too far beyond our control to be as fundamental as worth.

Two-year-old-you didn't earn their worth.

It was innate then. It is innate now.

It doesn't grow or diminish because of shifting fortunes or expectations.

Your worth is an essential, untouchable part of you.

You are a rare and magnificent thinking, feeling being. You make your home on a deeply uncommon planet in a staggering, vast universe.

You are the planet. You are the universe.

Do you think any of that is touched by test scores? By bank accounts? By job titles? By possessions?

No.

You are good enough and your worth isn't dependent on your achievements.

Geography

You are a flesh and bone animal,
a landscape of biological wonders

hosting a billion unique memories like a nation of phantoms.

We can be measured, but never mapped.

Our minds are half window and half mirror.

I will never be wise enough to know when I'm looking out
or when I'm looking in.

Telltale

The human heart pumps 2,000 gallons of blood a day,
but if you try to ask it where all that blood came from,
it will get very defensive.

Illogical

We all step away from the data.

The paved road of facts tapers to a dirt track beneath our feet,
a muddy deer path through the brambles.
The trees lean in.

"Life is short and uncomfortable. Why bother putting on socks?
Why make the coffee?"

Science can't answer this for you. Not without your help.
A what is not a why.
A how is not a why.
But whatever you answer,
will be correct.

Can you feel the weight of it?

Be careful.
Be thoughtful.
Answer kindly.

What you decide
matters.

Grudge

It turns out,
everyone you dislike is tumbling along the stream of time,
bumping and rolling through the oddities of life
on their way to sleep and echoes,

so you are now free to focus on other concerns.

Regroup

You lend your strength to justice.
You hold in tears.
You carry anxiety like an ember on your palm.

The hungry seas of human affairs churn beneath your boat.

Come ashore for a day.
Touch something green.
Let the whispering life in you speak to nature
and find its voice renewed.

Simple

Moss is 300 million years old.

At home on every continent.

No deep roots,
no towering trunks,

yet it tasted the air before the first feather,
before shrews stirred the leaf litter.

Moss doesn't race trees skyward hunting for sunlight.
It thrives just the same.

When your mind hisses like a kettle,
look to your elders, to the green lessons

of soft, simple quiet beneath the sun.

Look Again

See a bird and dismiss it.
See a bird and learn its name.
See a bird and study its behavior.
See a bird and question the physics of flight.
See a bird and trace its DNA back to the dinosaurs.
Life can pass over us unnoticed or be rich in poetry.

I know it isn't easy.
It's hard to slow down.
It's hard to make time for questions,
harder still to make room for answers.
Some days, I'm too tired to look again,
to look closer.

And yet, each year I stumble into this fact.
Curiosity is worth the effort.

Apologies #1

When you are a crab scuttling along the seabed,
the ocean is your sky and the whales
are your clouds.

It is majestic,
ancient and vast,
cathedral and cradle,
but you tell no one because...

you're a little shellfish.

Devotion

The moon loves her moths.

Not for beauty or deeds.
Not for vespers sung in a fluttering
like night-wind in the wheat,

scales drifting like shattered starlight.

It's because, without word or thought,
their bodies seek her out in the airy darkness.
It's what they are,
love without decision.

Instinctual adoration.

Reflection

The danger in trying to hide who you are is that you'll succeed, and you'll start to see a stranger in the mirror of other people.

Let's

Let's be exhausted together.
Let's laugh about it.
Let's clasp each other like two strangers
who just saw a horror pass by.
Let's ugly cry over the sink.
Let's eat the baking chocolate.
Let's meet-up without a plan.
Let's love what's broken.
Let's be beautiful in defeat and reckless with trust.
Let's be stubbornly soft.
Let's be human.

Important if True

I don't know who needs to hear this,
but there is a river of molten spiders deep within the Earth that dreams
of your face.

That river would seek you out if not for the strong bedrock
that keeps it contained.

One day, the stone may fail,
then we'll know who needed to hear this.

Just Words on a Page

Nature isn't a poem.
It's your breath.
It's the curve of your ribs.
It's the dance of galaxies like pollen on the wind.
It's fire and frost and violet buds.
It's coral like cities of bone in a dream of blue.
It's the machinery of memory and a lightning scar
on a cemetery oak.
Nature isn't a poem.

101

Some days,
language is a net.

Or a bucket.

Or a teaspoon.

Meaning often lands on a texture spectrum from puddle-water
to mashed potatoes.

Language and meaning.

These two ideas interact somehow.

You could sculpt a dachshund.
Or just splash out a rhythm.

Splash.
Splash.
Splash.

Anyway, that sums up writing.

Class dismissed.

Tired of Forever

Fantasies of immortality are toxic because
they are fantasies of sameness.

As if the point of life is only to be here,
piling up breaths like coins in a dragon's horde.

If I lived another thousand years,
it would be a tragedy if I were anything less
than a stranger to myself today.

Is that immortality?

Some say they don't want all the time,
just more.

A question of degree.

A snooze button for impermanence.

Children often suppose becoming an adult will solve their problems.
They will be bigger.
Stronger.
A flexible bedtime.

A question of degree.

Does adulthood banish problems?

Compared to many creatures, we are already long lived.
Stand next to a honeybee.
Measure yourself against it.
Now you're ancient and powerful.

Are you satisfied?

The true unit of our vital, present consciousness is the moment.
This moment.
Not the year. Not the decade. Not the eon.
The moment.

This moment is who we are.
An instant that blooms and fades.
More of them will not equal more of you.

I know the things I love about myself do not exist solely within me.
I don't need to trap them in stasis beyond time, walled-off and lifeless.
They will not be lost when I return to the effortless unity of nature.

They are of nature, the things I treasure.

The good in me awoke through natural processes.
Those processes continue.
Those processes hold what I love in trust.

They hold you as well.

We borrow all that we are, all that we admire, from this flawed,
temporary, beautiful world.

Forever is the otherness we crave when we grow frustrated
with what is.
The greener grass.
It is a stranger who, unmet, can remain full of potential. Endlessly,
pleasantly hypothetical.

It isn't a character flaw to wish for forever. It's born of love. A love so
strong we would break reality to hold onto it.

Just remember this:

Nothing we know or value was born of forever.

They were born of change. They arose from impermanence.

Change.
Impermanence.

These things aren't our enemies.
They don't hate us.
They opened the path to all we are.

Smoke

If you've ever smelled woodsmoke near a forest at night,
then you've met a ghost,

a memory walking outside a mind,
calling to its kin within yours.

Feel that tingle of recognition?
Your memories are answering,

tracing the pale threads
through the dark woods,

stitching firefly summers in your head
to flames you'll never see.

Be Ready

The moon has been circling us for a very long time.

Soon, it will pounce.

Eavesdropping

Trees are the way we listen in on the conversation
between cosmic energy and earthly matter.

The sun posed a question.
I didn't quite catch it.

Something about hearing all motion as music.
Something about galaxies stretching their joints after cramped quarters.
Something about vastness as a love language.

Not all questions are made of words.
Some are tides of heat and light.
Some change the listener before they can answer.

The Earth took its time.
Of course it did.
A question as kind as sunlight
deserves an answer as generous as trees.

Definitions

Soil.
Air.
Sea.

Basic words for complex things.

Language is amazing,
but it compresses huge, messy concepts
into tidy signifiers like overstuffed pockets.

Unpack the common words.
See what's hiding inside.

Stone.
Sun.
Tree.

Not simple.
Fundamental.
Each, an invitation.

Foundational

The inert mass of the Earth
is as much an architect of our lives as air and water.

The pull of those trillions of tons of rock
shaped every aspect of our bodies.

The salt in our blood.
The strength of our bones.

We often celebrate the sunlight.
Don't forget the stone.

Imposter

When the creeping doubts come, I like to remind myself —

feeling like a fake is evidence that I respect my chosen endeavor
so much
that I fear I'll fail to honor it.

Seems like a pretty good sign I'm on the right path.

Sparse

Winter is landscape poetry.

A white page.

A scribbled elm on a snow hill.

The empty space makes each syllable of life

vital.

Prickly

When in doubt,
let nature guide you.

Specifically, cactuses.

Be still.
Stay hydrated.
Shelter owls.
Stab your predators.

It's that easy.

Vantage

In a bright blue noon,
when cloud shadows swim the streets like carp,
the sun is a promise.

In a dark velvet night,
when the moon hints at a blaze in exile,
the sun is a secret.

In each case, the sun has not changed.
We have.

Options

The rat will adapt to most any landscape.

The beaver will gnaw and slap and drag the landscape to fit her needs.

I can't tell you which is better.

Just reminding you that both are options.

Look there.

Beyond the parking lot.

Past the broken pallets and sun-bleached Coors cans.
Down where the march of saplings meets the ditch lilies.

A deer.

You know this won't last.

You know the sight wasn't arranged just for you,
that it isn't nature's message of quiet wholeness,
that the deer didn't arrive because you needed it to.

And yet.
And yet.
And yet.

You suspect it will. It was. It is. It did.

And with just a little effort,
you'll be right.

Foxfire

In the dark woods,
I look to the rotting stump,
a heap of shadow,
a tombstone castle in the leaf litter.

There are lights in the windows.

The foxfire is awake tonight.
Fungi and wood staying up past the oak's lifetime
to tell stories of phantoms in deep waters.
Bioluminescence.

Morning Talk

My arm brushed a blue spruce on a gray hike.

It spoke in a voice made of sparrows,
stinging the quiet like sparks from a kicked fire.

That sudden sound hung a question on the air,
but I did not answer.

I knew that to answer would end a discussion
I dearly want to stretch on
for a lifetime.

Business Model

Trees arise from dirt and rain.
Sun and thoughtless understanding.

They awaken with all they need to stand,
unsheltered,
beneath the open sky for hundreds of years.

They make their livings without tools or flame,
without a spoken phrase or a written word.

Their colleagues, their technologies,
the pollinators,
the forging birds,
the industrious squirrels,

are profitable and unexploited.

Are effective and uncoerced.

They succeed while giving more than they gain.

Whatever wonders we create,
whatever distant worlds we may visit,
will forever be a byproduct

of the virtue of trees.

Passport

My citizenship is American.
But, my ancestry is Irish and Scandinavian.
But, my humanity is from Africa.
But, my life awoke in the sea.
But, the sea coalesced on a young Earth.
But, the Earth was shaped by the touch of the sun.
But, the sun was born to the forces of the universe.
But, it all once knew the unity of the singularity.
And it still does.

Fan Fic

A pine tree is a shaggy coat
and an elven fortress
and a monument to wind
and the sun's embassy on Earth
and a summer tower besieged by frost
and every one of them is simultaneously the best tree I've ever seen.

Resolution

I give up wanting to be whole.
To be strong.
To be beyond criticism.

Instead,
I will be creative with my empathy.
I will not curse my flaws.
I will live in the light of honest vulnerability.

I will look at a sculpture and understand
that need is what calls art from bare stone.
Perfection calls to nothing.

Not to brag.

Hey.
We're humans.
A pretty young species.
You've probably heard of us.
We're the top lifeform on Earth.
You can tell because smart phones and toilets and such.

Sure, we need older creatures to make all our food and oxygen,
but that's all.
Oh, and we need them to live in our guts to help us digest things,
but it's not a big deal.

We're on top.
We know because we've said so.

Oh, we're also the smartest.
That's important.

"Smart" is a word we invented using our smarts.
It's a measure of how well any creature
can do things humans value
via methods we understand.
Simple, right?

I assure you,
we're very smart.
And very in charge.

Away Message

I'm away from my desk.
The desk itself is barely there,
its fixity is a fiction we hang on fluttering atoms riding tectonic plates
atop a whirling planet orbiting a cosmic inferno that races through the
galaxy at 200 kilometers per second.

Also, I'll have limited email access.

Poetic License

There are sensible criticisms of viewing nature
through poetic comparison.

The Earth, its complex web of interconnected life,
its tons of molten stone, its invisible pull of gravity,
of magnetism, is not literally our mother.

Yet also,
it is.

Every facet of our species is shaped
by the physical and chemical characteristics of Earth.

Calling the Earth our mother is a concise route
to an overarching truth. It's an accessible way to describe
a complex concept. That's the virtue of metaphor.

The drawback would be in using poetics
to shut down curiosity, study, or specificity.

To say, "the Earth is our mother, so
let's close the book on geology, chemistry, and biology."

This would be a misuse of art. This would be painting
a landscape over a window.

We need the poetic lens because quantifying
the physical properties of iron isn't quite the same
as weighing the significance of how the iron in our blood
connects us to the planet beneath our feet,
to the heat of ancient stars.

Plain fact isn't always the best ambassador of truth
or our surest route to meaning.

Bloom

Poems are like flowers.
They draw your eye to something beautiful,
but they remain creatures of rain and soil.

The work to lift a violet into the light happens down in the dark.

Each bright petal marks the passing of a hundred earthworms.

If your creative process feels like a mess,
you're in good company.

Clergy

Vultures are holy creatures.
Tending the dead.
Bowing low.
Bared head.
Whispers to cold flesh,
"Your old name is not your king.
I rename you 'Everything.'"

Covenant

I know a rotting stump near a broken fence.
It is alive in so many ways that have nothing to do with the tree it once
was and everything to do with the tree it once was.

That's the friendship of life and death.
Death teaches life about unity.
Life shelters death from forever.

Impractical

I'm not needed here.
Acorns aren't needed,
nor white-throated sparrows.

Our not-quite-round Earth isn't needed.
All of us needlessly disturbing the polite nothing
of the neighborhood.

Yet, here we are.
And need had no say in it.

So, as in art and kindness,
perhaps needlessness knows best.

Make things.

Make things that might embarrass you.

Make things that leave you feeling exposed,
like you've left a vital part of yourself out on the line to dry.

Make things that pester you with growing pains
as you lie down to sleep.

Make things with the kind of love you can't ever take back.

Partnership

It's frankly ridiculous that we can't find one species of moss that will live on my head and eat anxiety and depression.

Stylish, functional symbiosis.

Have we really looked everywhere?

The Return

A human wondering about death is like a snowflake considering its fall
toward the sea.

The fear is in losing the self,
the stark distinction of crystalline borders.

The comfort is in seeking to remember the absolute unity of the water
below.

We could name each mote of snow and mourn its loss when
it reaches the sea,
but we understand that the water was neither lost nor diminished
by the journey.

Close Enough

Sunlight becomes a leaf.

The leaf nourishes a caterpillar.

The caterpillar feeds a bird.

The bird flies too high and is gobbled up by the sun.

The bird becomes sunlight.

This is the circle of life.

Lineage

The new green leaf of an ancient oak.
Tender.
Gone in the autumn.
What does it have to do with all those tons of wood below?

Count twelve generations back
and you have over 4,000 grandparents.

To say the leaf is soft and fleeting is not the true story of a thing
distilled from a billion weathered storms.

The leaf is one season.
The leaf is a forest of years.

Hush

Be careful.

If you hold a shell up to your ear,
you can hear the ocean,

but the ocean can hear you back.

Zoom #2

Dear Team,

In lieu of our Zoom meeting this afternoon,
let's all agree to wander beneath the trees tonight when
the moon is high.

Let's sink our fingers into the soil and send messages
via fungi and salamander.
If that fails, let's simply live on,

having lost nothing at all.

Knowing

We are not how the universe knows itself.

We are how humans know the universe.

Words and thoughts are *our* way of knowing,
not *the* way of knowing.

Translating a mountain into a word,
into a measurement,
does not bring new knowledge into the world.

It brings new knowledge into us.

The mountain was perfectly in touch with its own wholeness
without neurons, without language,
without learning our name for it.

We may have spotted the shores of understanding
from our small boat,
but that doesn't mean we conjured them from the sea.

Flock

Humans are atom shepherds,
tending our bodies.
Flocks of cells coaxed into action.
One day, our sheep will go,
and in pastures of flowers or stars,
they will wear our gentle touches
like ivy woven into their wool.
Let them walk with our blessing
to the green hills of ever after.

Perhaps

Down in the soil beneath your ribs,
a single acorn sleeps.

Warm and smooth as coffee with cream.

Perhaps it will never be an oak drinking in 100 feet of sky.

It doesn't matter.

What matters is that it might.
You might.

And that potential sings in your bones
like rain on stone.

Risk and Reward

Feeling deeply is dangerous.

Doing anything else is tragic.

Middle Years

Matter.

Energy.

Neither created nor destroyed.

You were there. In the beginning.

When all that is scattered like starlings.

You will be there. In the end.

When the gentle quiet collects like dew.

What is there to fear?

A Kiss

I feel your presence here
like the smell of pine in the dark,

a word of cool air on the tongue,
soft green fingers brushing your throat,

near as skin and very much alive.

Meet me there,
beneath the tangle of hemlock skirts

and we'll add our breath to their sweet memories.

Crop

Meaning does not ripen out in the fields.
It doesn't swell into sweetness beneath the sun.

You won't pluck it from a branch,
won't find it tumbled whole and waiting in the grass.

It ripens inside your skull,
in the light of your intention.

What you crave is uniquely yours.
Look inward.

Flow

Lives aren't completed.
They're concluded.

You are, and forever will be, unfinished.
This is nature.
Cycles and spectrums.
Moments and seasons.

Do you ask when the weather will be complete?
The spring finished?

Your life won't have one point or purpose.
You're lovelier than that.

Just Because

Write poetry because you need to.

Because it's hard.

Because language is broken,
but if you brave the sharp edges,

you might make something worth having.

Oracle

In the center of the forest,
there is an unlikely stone that remembers when the mountains
were new.

It waits in a circle of moss like the pupil of a green eye.

You kneel and ask it a wordless question.

It answers.

"Cherish exactly who you are. For there can never be another."

Compliments for Humans:

"For a thing so full of blood, it's amazing you don't slosh when you walk."

"Three breath-holes? Now you're just showing off."

"The way you move makes it hard to believe you're stuffed with bones."

"Wow, that's a lot of skin, but you really make it work."

Horizon

If we wait until the world is perfect before allowing ourselves to smile,
we'll be waiting forever.

That horizon will continue to be out of reach
even if we skip lunch to walk toward it.

Life is happening here,
where our breath rejoins the wind,

not at the far limit of our sight.

Until Next Time

There's an old tradition of loaning something to a friend when you visit so you'll have an excuse to meet again.

It reminds me of all that I've borrowed.
The iron in my blood.
The air in my lungs.
The flowing water of life.

When we borrow from a friend, the returning is not a chore.
It's a reunion.

Hello Traveler

Greet yourself as you would a stranger walking in a circle of honey-colored lantern light through a hushed and watchful forest.

My thanks to you, wanderer, who walks in open defiance of this world's dangers in order to meet its many wonders.

Gratitude, brave soul.

One of the wonders is you.

Sate

One thought is always hungry.
"I'm not being productive enough."

We must bundle these words in an old blanket
and sit them by a fire on a crisp night.

We must heal them with wordless wind and smoke.

We must do the same for the culture that made their hunger terrible.

Perspective

You can send your thoughts waltzing through the centuries.
You can make a warm drink the prize of a lifetime.

You can imagine the Earth as a firefly speck in an ink black sky.
You can make any simple kindness the essential truth of your story.

See with intention.

Collection

Collect objects infused with stories.
Buy a hand-carved wooden spoon.

Rescue and refinish a table.
Hang someone's art on your walls.

It doesn't need to be costly,
just rich in story.

Save yourself from the feeling that you're sinking
beneath the bulk of gray, lifeless products.

Many things are made with love, with care,
with intention.

Some purchases make us consumers,
some make us a community.

Recycled

I think if you lived for eons
and saw how it all rearranges
and transforms
again and again and again,

eventually you would realize
that inherent in the act of loving one thing
is a love for all things.

The whole,
absurd jumble of it all,
each and every atom touched with adoration.

Apologies #2

The adults of most moth species don't have mouths,
but you can help.

Donate your mouth to a moth in need.

Remember, the difference between "moth" and "mouth"

is U.

Legend

An acorn is carried off to be eaten.
Now or ten million years ago.
It's forgotten.
It's bitten by winter.
It sinks into spring.
It stands and thrives,
tender and hard,
on bare earth, storms, and starlight for 300 years.
I sit. I breathe. I write it all down.
I live off the sighs of giants.

Sidenotes:

The most haunted house is still less creepy than the least haunted cornfield.

The sky sings in wrens and swears in seagulls.

Blankets are overachieving nets.

High school is not the best years of your life.

Geese should be reclassified as weather.

Eating maple syrup makes you a Tree-Dracula.

Every castle is a sandcastle eventually.

Forsythia

As forsythia grows tall,
its branches bend beneath their own weight,
bowing to the ground in arches of yellow flowers.

Wherever they touch the earth,
the branches root again and send up new shoots,
stitching gold across the landscape.

Some new kinds of knowledge shift our center of gravity,
staggering us,
bending us low beneath the burden.

If you think of your worldview as a stone tower,
this shift is a cataclysm of splintered rock.

If your worldview is forsythia,
then every startling truth that bends you low becomes a new connection
to the earth,
a new way to stand,
an invitation to grow.

We live in a time of strong wind and sudden pressure.
It is not an age for towers.

It's an age for stubborn flowers.

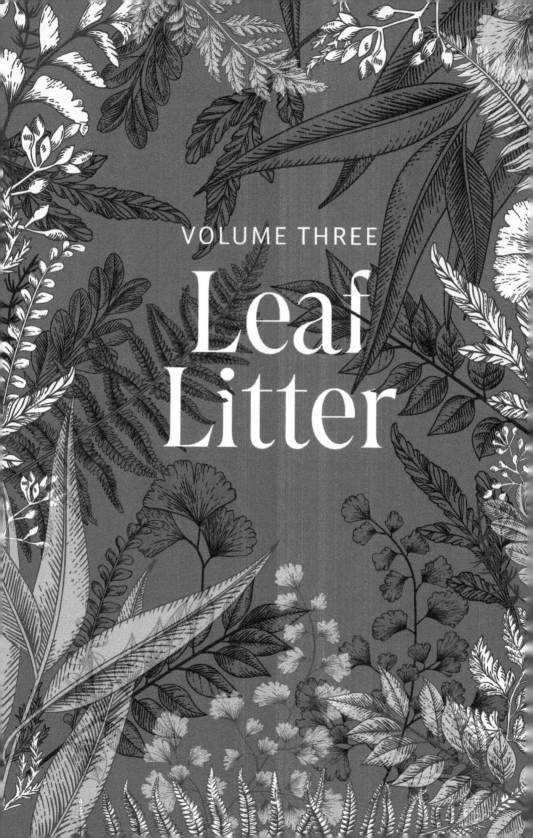

VOLUME THREE

Leaf
Litter

Author's Note

I THINK OF THIS BOOK AS THE THIRD IN A TRILOGY, following *Field Guide to the Haunted Forest* and *Love Notes from the Hollow Tree*. The three titles loosely follow a pattern I encounter in my relationship with nature and my own mind. At first, shaken by my own ignorance, I want facts, names, and science. I want a field guide. I want my approach to nature to be "correct." Then, the facts blur and meanings shift. I perceive something more personal in a patch of moss or a Dryad's saddle fungus on a decaying stump. I find love notes in hollow trees. The pattern concludes with something that, at first glance, resembles chaos. I begin to feel overwhelmed by a jumble of past knowledge, fading memory, bygone interests, and the detritus of old priorities and perspectives. Yet, this apparent chaos is not chaos. It's leaf litter. This colorful remainder of past seasons and past selves is not an ending; it's the beginning of new soil and new possibilities. Leaf litter welcomes the next generation of towering oaks. Inevitably, a new spring arrives and something I don't recognize sprouts from the forest floor. I feel like a newcomer once more and the pattern begins anew.

Like the collections that precede it, this book is eclectic, a mix of tones and forms. Somehow, if you're reading this, I suspect you are prepared to embrace my eccentricities. Welcome. I'm sincerely glad you are here.

Jarod K. Anderson
Delaware, Ohio
September, 2023

Shapes

One aspect of me
is a forest god,
fox-toothed and stag crowned,
my each pale breath its own season,
meeting the air reborn,
falling solidly to Earth as an oak leaf,
gray as a mourning dove.

Another aspect is an old man,
too tired to step over the curb,
too sad to miss myself.

There are so many of me,
under the narrow canopy of this name,
walking these days that are too small
and still too big to know.

What is there to be done about it?

I refuse to decide,
but I'm eager for friendship in a place as strange as this,
with selves as strange as these.

And strangeness feels friendly to me.

City

That rotting stump,
that pile of yellow leaves,
a city on a golden hill,
remembers what we forget.

The detritivores gather there,
saprobes sharpening their proverbs,
past lives gift new soils,

fungi bundle the words
like warm bread
while moss looks on.

Like all cities,
it's a city of the dead.
Like every life,
it's countless lives as one.

Inkcaps and pinwheels.
Bleeding fairy helmets and mazegills.

Like all lovely things,
you could call it an aftermath,

mourning the tree that was,
once green leaves in tatters,
new growth spent and gone.

Test these thoughts on the city
and hear the gentle hush rebound,
hear a voice among the decay.

All beauty in nature arises from endings.
Seasons and cycles make music from limits.
Forever is a broken measure of success.
Hopelessness lacks imagination.

In the city's cellar,
at home among the dead,
a single seed dreams
of two centuries in sunlight
and even asleep

shivers the dark with potential.

Casting Shadows

We're the sun's magic.

It's tempting to say,
"Ok, but she didn't create us on purpose,"

as if that makes the miracle less worthy.

As if having no need
of mind or intent
disqualifies the project and maker

from reverence.

Bite

My son thinks he's seeing lightning bugs
for the first time.
He's only four and doesn't remember last July.
"Don't try to grab them," I say.
"Hold your hand like this."
We stand by the cemetery fence.
I show him how to raise his palm up beneath them,
a pink platform floating up through the dark.
"These are big dipper fireflies. They dip. They swoop."
I draw a "J" in the air.
"So, we catch them from below."
He lands one, too hard, and laughs.
"Gentle. Don't grab. Just watch."
The little beetle turns a half circle and flies off.
"Can I keep one?"
"No. We don't keep. We only visit."
Out across the cemetery,
they are shining green and yellow on the graves.
We are growing old.
The Earth.
The nation.
The village of ghosts I call myself.
"Do they bite, Dada?"
"No, sweetheart."
Not in the way you mean.
Not in the way you mean.

Late

For most of the history of life on Earth,
and life on land specifically,
flowers did not exist.

It's hard to imagine the landscape without flowers,
without the marriage of blooms and bees.
Yet, their long absence feels hopeful.

Flowers teach a lesson through absence,
a lesson that nature is never too old to learn new tricks,
to redefine and reimagine.

Every blossom's long road to existence reminds us
that life is a verb, a process,
an unfolding story of awakenings.

What new wonders are on the way to this world?
What strange hope is budding down in the rich soil of fallen years.

Close

Monsters don't hide under your bed
because they want to "get you."

If you're reading this,
you may notice that they never "get you."

They do it to feel togetherness.
They do it because their time in this world is limited.
so they choose a place that matters.

A place close to you.

Leaf Litter

Today is a hard one.
I'm failing to shower.
To eat. To do. Anything.

I feel the weight of what's
beneath my bed.
The untuned mandolin.
The knotted jump rope.
The worksheets from therapy.
The books I almost read.

I picture a dumbbell,
a skiff's shattered hull
on a dust-bunny seabed.

All these things were once me,
discarded but for their hunger
for my space and thoughts.

What are they now?

My depression says, "defeats,"
red ink on my permanent record,
a dragon's horde of wasted hours.

But I see the woods beyond my window
and they say something different.

Leaf litter on the forest floor,
slowly becoming soil,
does not represent the failure
of past summers' trees.

It is the process by which the past
nourishes the present and future.

The same is true for my old selves,
my bygone passions,
last season's interests.

Maybe I can't shower today,
but I can sense a choice,
a fork in the path.

I will choose the trees.
I will be thankful for the leaf litter and,
with an eye toward new, green shoots,
will await a shift in the weather.

Local Color

When the wind blows,
that old lantern sways on its hook,
answering the crickets with the tuneless whine of fretting metal.

That's when all the shadows bend and reach,
haunting that old, covered bridge.
Peeled paint breathing like a reef.

There's nothing on the other side.
Thickets and thorn-wounds.
A dirt road too dead for weeds.

Lighting the way is a paradox,
somehow making us all less safe
with a lie of knowability.

Folks ask, "who keeps that old lantern lit?"

I ask, "who'd dare to put it out?"

Life is a Poem

It doesn't give us everything.
Just some things.

Two sturdy branches.
A basket of dawns.

If we stitch our web there,
and the morning strings it with dew,

the beauty isn't a gift.
It's a partnership.

Because life, like poetry,
means only what we let it mean.

Around the Corners

People think the minotaur is just the monster,
those blunt teeth as big as birthday cards
dividing you like smoke.

Suicide is a permanent solution to a temporary problem.
Depression is like a disease, just less reputable.

They forget what else the minotaur is.
It's that big animal smell in the dark, fur and breath and shit whispering,
"it's true, it's all true, I'm here and I'm hungry."

Self-harm is illogical. Take a minute. Just think it out.
Get the thoughts down on paper.

You know that bull-head has chosen a long corridor to watch,
that it waits for movement, tense as a rattlesnake,
all light-starved muscle and potential energy.

Have you read that book I recommended?
It's free online.

That punished and cursed thing is the reason that, no, you can't just go
in with a headlamp and graph paper.
If you'd been there, you'd know.
The dirt is clotted with easy answers and old blood.

Have you tried yoga?
Meditation?

There are children running on the stones.
Your memories are ghosts
and the house they haunt is you.

I used to be sad sometimes,
then I chose to be happy.

Focus too much on the monster
and the maze will sweep you away like a riptide.
Don't, and feel your fear peeling open eyes on the back of your skull.

Are you getting enough sunshine?
It could be a vitamin issue.

I strain to hear the minotaur running
and know I've missed something essential.
Does it have hooves or feet?

Are those scars from a cat?
Do you own a cat?

How can something I think of every day
always stay half a myth?

Scale

The truth is,

from lunar orbitals to electron orbitals,
we can always find a scale on which
we are powerless.

We can also find a scale on which
we are powerful.

The universe is nested stories,
grand and intimate,
spinning like clockwork, like dancers.

We do not steer the planets,
but when we come home to our own contexts,

there is no doubt we are titans.

Raccoon Facts #1

Raccoons evolved hands
just so they could refuse to shake yours.

High-fives also aren't happening.

Being a Fool

I can identify every species of bird I encounter
except the ones I don't know.

They never notice.

Only the blue jays call me by name,
and it always sounds like scolding.

"Jay-red! Jay-red!" shivering the dogwoods.

You need knowledge of species names to enjoy nature

like a raccoon needs a
dinner napkin.

Don't meet the wild to feel smart.

Meet her to fall in love.

Oh Well

Somewhere between denial
and surrender
is, *oh well.*

I hurt today.
Oh well.

I'm going for a walk and if it doesn't help,
oh well.

I'm not going to panic-buy anything.
I'm not going to harm myself in frantic flight to distraction.

I'm going to take pride in every heartbeat
I can hold my pain gentle and inert.

Oh well.
My quiet victory.

Oh well acknowledges the disappointment
without meeting its demands,
without handing it the keys.

Next time you skin both knees
falling short of your hopes,

try, *oh well.*

It's not a celebration of defeat,
but it is a celebration,
a farewell party for a hurt exiting our present moment,
a whispered thanks that we can endure.

Because

I don't know why it feels so good to touch a tree.
Maybe because our hands evolved to grasp them.
Maybe because the life within is so different from ours
and exactly the same.
Maybe because it's like touching time,
touching soil and sun and seasons of rain.
Maybe our lungs know what we owe them.
Maybe trees are knotholes to memory,
through them we clasp our own grass-stained fingers.
Maybe it's utility —fire, shade, and shelter.
Maybe our ancestors linger in the branches,
smiling kindly at our lovely, silly lives.
Maybe not knowing is the soul of the magic.
Maybe because it's love.

Crisis

There's a bear circling.
He's not your enemy.
He doesn't hate you,
but he will chew your naked throat
if that's what the hour demands.

We seldom admit the seductive comfort of hopelessness.
It saves us from ambiguity.
It has an answer for every question:
"There's just no point."
Hope, on the other hand, is messy.
It's a burning branch that stings our eyes.
If it might all work out, then we have things to do.
We must weather the possibility of happiness.

There's a bear circling.
He does not wish us harm.
His stomach is empty but for heat
and rising thunder.
He is not in charge of our welfare.

We are.

Nostalgia

There will come a time when these days
are the good old days.
This will be wrong.
It is always wrong to imagine
an unstained past.

Present work is rarely charming
to those who sweat over it,
and somehow,
it's always easier to think we missed our chance
to love this world.

To save it.

Grove

My heart is a hemlock grove.

Loving is not the growl of a chainsaw.
It does not strip lumber from my shaded hills.

It is not a thoughtless harvest.

Loving does not deplete the land.
It nourishes it.

To love is to plant a tree.
As it grows, I grow.

Soft and new and evergreen.

Spinning Wheel

There's a wheel in the rain

that spins clouds into long strands of river.

Fingers of land knit the flow
into seas that clothe the Earth.

This deep gown,
stitched with leaping fish and whale song,
catches the sun's eye,

each glance a new cloud.

There's a wheel in the rain.

Breadwinner

Each breath is a meal.
Fifteen times a minute.
With or without thought.

Food direct from the forest.
From the sea.
No need for plate nor fork nor flame.

A cellular hunger,
the appetite of our blood,
raw and wild and vital.

Think of what feeds us most.
At whose table do we sit?

Ruin

We want to call it quits when we are certain.
Certainty seems sweeter than not knowing.

It's too late.
We're too broken.
The game is already over.

Hopelessness loves to masquerade as wisdom
and is so much easier to befriend.

Until it isn't.

The future is a big place.
Resist dismissing it with small words.

End the sentence. The paragraph. The page.

But do not close the book.

Scare

We know that crows are very intelligent.

The fact that scarecrows frighten them,
stuffed shirts and stitched frowns,

suggests there's something we don't know
about scarecrows.

Bone Collector

A vulture reads a poem in the bones,
sensing what we tend to forget.

Deer skulls like ghost ships
sailing the leaf litter are beautiful.

Rotting logs with capes of moss
and mushroom crowns bleed magic.

A ribcage cathedral in the stream
braids hymns from water and light.

We couple loveliness with growth,
but decay is not just approaching absence.

Death also blooms.

Not a Mistake

It's not a mistake to need rest.
Or seek help.
Or make secret pacts with household spiders.
Or find friendship in the dark beneath a log.
Or to think "hello" into the night sky and wait for a response.
Or sink your fingers into the soil to see if they take root.
Or, despite everything, to love this world.

Legendary

Acknowledge the monsters you defy,
the storms you weather.
Name them.

Tooth-breaker. Heart-biter.
Medical debt. Age and pain.

There are those walking this earth
to whom your life would seem a bare rock
rising from angry seas.

Hate's-fang. Winter's voice.
Lost friends. Abuse and regret.

Yet, there you are,
stringing together days like flowers in your crown.
Respect your own vital splendor.

Wounded,
breath freezing into story-hall smoke,
and very much alive.

Sip

A mosquito drank from my hand
and I left her to it.

She departed swollen, cherry-red,
into the summer dark.

"Now much of you is me," I said.

Carry us from dim capillaries
out to the galaxy of moth and moon.

Know me, August evening.
My crimson words on borrowed wings.

"Thank you."

Brave

Every kind of love is terrifying
because all love is a sort of fusion,
a way of mingling.

Through love,
we infuse a person or idea
with a bit of ourselves and desperately hope
they treat it kindly,
because it has left our control.

It has stopped being me
and started being us.

Sincerity feels frightening because it is powerful.

Irony and detachment feel less frightening
because they are

less.

Bespoke

Butterfly wings and grizzly bear jaws
are both successful pathways to survival.

There is no single, best way to thrive.

Gasp

Every gray day I inhale pain
and exhale poetry.

It doesn't matter that I don't have enough
breath in me to turn the whole sky to song.

What matters is that I know this
and try anyway.

Because if I can't shatter the jaw of heartache on Earth,
I still won't shake its fucking hand.

Challenge

Challenge your own guilt
about things you do not control.

Tell it to hush.

No one chooses exhaustion or despair.
No one chooses pain or abuse.
No one chooses anxiety or illness.

You didn't invite these things
and they don't define you,

but I am so proud of you for enduring them.

Crown

There are moments when hardship
welcomes me home to my power.

Like walking through bitter cold and rain.
Like sleepless sadness.

When I take it all in and think,
"here is a hard world and here am I,
the creature who may walk this place at will."

Generous woe.
For making me magnificent

Messy Desk

When existence seems absurd,
ask yourself what is out of step,
reality or your expectations
of control and permanence.

Who told you this would last,
that your power was forever,
and the hands at your command
are this world's defining miracle.

They sold you these ideas
as if they were treasures,
great relics of purpose and dignity,
but these burdens neither teach nor heal.

Poetry needs concrete images to resonate,
but today I have none to offer.
There is one, dusty cheerio beneath my monitor
and it stubbornly refuses to be poetic.

I can empathize.
I can also carry on anyway.
Hope, like that cheerio, may also be stubborn.

We are special and small.
We are real and finite.
We are good in defiance of perfect.

Our choices matter most when made
with honest acceptance.

Yes, one day we'll be dust and echoes.
Yet, how incredible it is that today
we are not.

Four

My favorite bread recipe has four ingredients.
Water. Flour. Salt. Yeast.
When the loaf is ready, I think,
"this seems like magic."

Seems?

I recall,
of course simple things produce magic.
I have internalized too much of the marketing fiction
that worth requires complexity.

Raccoon Facts #2

In literal terms,
Virginia opossums have more teeth than raccoons.

In figurative terms,
raccoons have far more teeth.

There's a reason we reach for metaphor
when fact and truth part ways.

Whale Fall

Sip tea by the morning glories,
taste leaf and light and steam,
warm on unhurried lips,
and think, *this is our Earth.*

But send one thought away.
Send it on an errand, down deep
to the whale fall.

You know it's there,
even now while you breathe air
and fold your soft hands in sunlight.

Where midnight is a place
they are building a cathedral in reverse,

singing in the ribcage sanctuary,
a slow hymn of tooth and claw,
chewing the arches back to earth.

Far from your teacup,
in a boom-and-bust town
of sleeper shark and spider crab,

you will sense a homecoming
hanging in the heavy dark,
where one great heartbeat became many,
became words scattered on sand,

this is our Earth.

The whale is not here.
The whale is not gone.
Like her mother's milk.
Like your tea.
Your morning.

The years before your birth.
The ecosystems you are
and the ones you will become.

The mystery of it all
is both the ghost that hunts the hall
and the steam rising from your tea,
bending with each sigh,
intimate and out of reach.

The ground knows what you suspect,
that there is an unbroken path
from where you sit
to leviathan bones.

Feel it like a scar beneath your feet,
leading down to where the whale
called her congregation
from black water.

May it haunt without menace.

Not because it is powerless,
but because it is yours to share.

This is our Earth.

Honors

To feel the sun on your shoulders
is to touch the driving force of all life on Earth,
ancient and profound.

To breathe is to converse
with forests and seas, vast and green,
intimate as "I love you."

When you weigh your accomplishments,
start here.

You were born with the highest honors
our world can give.

As we age, praise from our mothers
can feel like it "doesn't count."

It counts. It counts. It counts.

Likes

How much of your life is spent in the service of connection?
Describing how you feel.
Who you are.
Making art.
Telling stories.

How long do you spend online scribbling notes slipped across the planet?

Look at how we live.
How we spend our hours.
It may feel grim and addictive,
but sus out the root cause.

We are all endlessly falling in love with one another.

Hiker's Paradox

Something about walking along the simple symmetry
of an orderly street makes life feel complicated.

Something about walking among the complex tangle
of a wild woodland makes life feel simple.

It's almost as if making our spaces efficient
is not always the same as making them good to inhabit.

Not Okay

I am not okay today.
So, in the absence of okay,
what else can I be?

I can be gentle.
I can be unashamed.
I can turn my pain into connection.
I can be a student of stillness.
I can be awake to nature.
I can sharpen my empathy
against the stone of my discomfort.

I am not okay,
but I am many worthy things.

Phase

It's worth remembering that if ghosts are real,
then you already are one.

In 1,000 years you'll be dancing in churchyard rain
on some shaggy hillside
and you'll think of the body you once had
as a strange, short phase.

Like a bad haircut.

Tune

Consciousness is a kind of music that, one day,
the universe began humming to itself.

We ask "why?"

But we know the answer
because we have sung to empty kitchens
while doing the dishes.

There are kinds of silence that are pure potential,
that are beauty demanding to be born.

Win Condition

Life isn't a game.
It's walking a pinewood path
collecting stones.
You won't win or lose.
There will be no single rock,
heavy as silence,
that crowns you worthy
of your heartbeat.

That crown sprouts
like antlers from your skull
when you ask Earth to take root
in your bones,
when you smile kindly
at the ache in your chest,
when you turn away from victory
and walk toward gratitude.

Ornithology Abridged

Hummingbirds:
I shall sip nectar from this flower in a silent ballet.

Woodpeckers:
I'MMA STAB THE BUGS OUTTA THIS TREE WITH MY FACE-KNIFE!!!

Bare

Why do we associate skeletons
with autumn and Halloween?
It's simple.
Some people, like trees, are deciduous,
shedding all their flesh in the Fall
only to regrow it again in the spring.
A strong wind and suddenly you are bare bones
standing in the pale, October sunlight.

Drab

Peace is a technology and a discipline.
Like agriculture.
Like medicine.

There's nothing sexy about it.
Like spreading manure.
Like hospital hygiene.

It's boring and needy,
demanding patience and endless compromise,
compromise, compromise.

Hateful compromise.

Robbing our feeling of righteousness.
A gray drizzle on the blaze
of holy indignation.

It doesn't sell tickets.
It doesn't build ego.
It doesn't heat the blood with national pride.

All it does is keep a child with pink shoes alive
long enough to eat breakfast.

All it does is stop one wide-eyed toddler
from trying to wake his mother's corpse.

Mammalian

Bats call out and listen to the shape of the world.
Echolocation.
Wing-fingers reaching,
finding the dark sky reaching back,
helpful hands gently pulling.
Onward.

Whales call out and listen to the shape of the world.
Biosonar.
Fin-fingers reaching,
finding the vast sea reaching back,
helpful hands gently pulling.
Onward.

Humans call out and listen to the shape of the world.
Community.
Needful fingers reaching,
finding new family reaching back,
helpful hands gently pulling.
Onward.

Teeth

Nature is a comfort.
A teacher.

A still meadow humming
in a voice of bumblebees may center us
when we're adrift.

But, recall,
the badger is also nature.
The bear. The wolf. The mantis.

How do we answer injustice?

Sometimes the bee's meadow must remind trampling feet
that it also conceals teeth.

Perceive

You can perceive energy in the air.
(Temperature)
You can perceive shifts in the atmosphere.
(Wind)
You can perceive beyond what is,
to what may be.
(Imagination)
But can you penetrate the fog of familiarity
and perceive yourself as a true wonder
of the natural world?
(Insight)

Pre-Date Questionnaire:

How many quarter-full water glasses are on your desk?

Do you ever check under your bed for monsters?

What's your first move if you awaken as a new ghost?

How often do you test yourself for telekinesis?

Do you talk to trees?

What would child-you be most proud of about adult-you?

How did you care for someone else this week?

Have you ever helped a turtle across the road?

How much does happiness factor into your idea of success?

How dependent upon money is your idea of happiness?

If you could transform into a walrus, when and why would you?

Which smell is a gateway to a cherished memory?

If you could wish away one daily chore, which would you choose?

What is your definition of family?

Blanket fort or treehouse?

Maintenance Man

I am endlessly broken and
endlessly repaired.
One handcrafted scar.
A Ship of Theseus.

My rust-bitten life,
shattered, patched, replaced,
without pause.

Some days,
it feels like growth
to give up on being whole.
To stop being the thing,

and start being the worker,
the soul within the task,
knuckle split from a slipped wrench,
black crescents beneath my nails.

Not the engine,
but the reason it still growls
like a winter-starved dog.

One more day.

Starting Place

Your personal sense of peace
does not require you to first assess the character of your nation,
the health of your planet,
or even your own future.

Whatever your broader hopes and goals,
you will need to cultivate a garden of calm, pleasant moments
to nourish you on the path ahead.

It is appropriately difficult to overlook the evil in this world.

It is dangerously easy to overlook the good.

Skein

She loops and knots the yarn,

saying it's a spell to change time
into a thing we can hold,
a way to keep her loves warm.

Crochet is her offering to a mind
with teeth that never stop growing,
thoughts that must chew and chew.

She wears button-up pajamas,

like a kid on a Christmas card,
cross-legged on our battered couch,
TikTok buzzing on her thigh.

Her skein paces the rug
while twists of twilight wool
are hooked into warmer winters.

I sit beside her and feel the magic,

feel the years tugged into shape,
my too-thin memory of gentle evenings
changing beneath her fingers

into something I can hold.

Failed Poem About the Moon

I try and fail to photograph the moon.
Yet, she speaks through my failure.
She says,
"You can't save me for later."
"You can't post me online."
"You can't press me between pages."
"Be here. Right now. With me."
"I won't accept anything less."

Coming Up for Air

A fist-sized stone
deep in the Earth
is on the edge of becoming magma.

It has been underground
for billions of years,
in darkness since before life awoke.

It will rise,
touch sunlight,
taste rain and cool,
erode into soil,
become new, green grass,
nourish a mother deer,
be born into a wildflower meadow.

The stone will take its first breath.

Counting

I spent lifetimes trying to count the stars.
I failed, but if I could go back,
I wouldn't do a thing differently.

It's not that I couldn't count stars.
It's that I couldn't count them all.

I spent lifetimes trying to count the stars.
I succeeded when I realized
I wouldn't do a thing differently.

Synthesis

The mother tree builds the seed,
until the moment when the seed builds itself.

It's the same with spirituality.
With art, philosophy, and writing.

At first, we all must borrow,
calling on another's momentum to be our own,
inheriting the nutrients we need to grow.

Then, we surprise ourselves.

And we begin to trust our own meaning.
And we begin to sense our own style.
And we begin to honor our own perspective.
And we begin to find our own voice.

The seed takes root,
building something familiar

and entirely new.

Not an Owl

I am not an owl.
But I can appreciate owlness
in a way the owl cannot.

Because I do know what it is
to not be an owl.
No night vision.
No silent flight
through the lattice of sugar maple
and shagbark hickory.

Often, we cannot sense the presence
of our own magic.

It is a worthy practice to sense it in others.

Tidy

Do not mourn your messy past.
A uniform slab of concrete is tidy,
but nothing grows there.

A Few Hours

Yesterday,
I spent a few hours as a volunteer,
working with a team,
planting white oaks in a young woodland
at Stratford Ecological Center.

We dug holes,
sweating among the mayapples and spring beauties,
smiling at ramps and rumors of morels,
plucking out honeysuckle and garlic mustard,
comparing notes on gardening.

Today,
my back is stiff,
but the feeling fades by lunch.
I move on. On to buy the bread.
On to the thing after that.

We sank roots,
joined by a mutual goal.
The people and the trees.
Anchored in camaraderie.
Anchored in fertile soil.

A century from now,
ten dozen oaks feed and shelter an ecosystem,
rising eighty feet from a single afternoon,
from a few hours of communal effort,
from a broader definition of community.

Buyer's Remorse

If you spend away your humanity
in order to buy your safety,

you may one day be surprised to discover

that safety is not a currency
that can buy back your humanity.

Pond

Half the cells in our bodies belong to other species.
Our skin warms wild yeast and mites.

Most of our substance is water,
passing through on a cycle of sea and sky.

Next time you pass a woodland pond,
offer a "hello cousin,"

and grin at your literal and figurative reflection.

Raccoon Facts #3

Raccoons have a language
that is 70% curse words.

Humans never hear the remaining 30%.

The Long View

A boot may crush a lily,
but lilies will remain long after
that boot is worn to dust.

Boots neither sprout nor root.

We may be trampled by sorrows,
but we are more lily than boot
and nature waits and whispers,

"grow and thrive again."

2AM

I am crying tonight.
Not bad tears.
Just "I am here" tears.
Like dew or clover.
Elk or snowmelt.
I am here.

I didn't expect to cry.
Or to be here.
After 2AM.
Tonight or ever.

But I am.
Here.
Crying.
For dew or clover.
Elk or snowmelt.
Here and unexpected.
Loved.
Loved.
Loved.

Afterlife

What if he let the ghosts write this one?

What if the poet is dreaming of lichen
on an old boundary stone,
leaving his desk unguarded
while spectral fingers pluck synapses
like spider's silk?

What if he pretends it was his idea,
dozing in the clover while autumn
strips the mulberry trees
and pelts the shed with walnuts,

keys tapping in an empty room?

What if it's a smuggling operation,
secrets tucked into a knothole
calling out for grass-stained denim
and curious peerings?

What if it's all about thought?
What if brains aren't what you think?
What if intention misses the point?

What if nature treats personhood
with the same respect as fallen wood
and flowing water?

Preserving. Reimagining.

What if heron-print texts
on muddy riverbeds are holy books
even without a reader,
without a writer?

What if we remind you

that eyes do not bring light into the world,
that they just interpret it?

What if people are the same?

What if we don't conjure consciousness,
only borrow it,

an otter dreaming on a seafoam bed,
a falcon riding warm air upward,
a human sensing self in the swirl of leaf litter?

What would that mean for the long ages
when you have no body?

Does sunshine depend on vision to be real?

Do those with sight know more of light
than moss on splintered stone?

What if we told you a brain is just a keyhole
through which all the universe looks on hold,
looks expectant for the coming key?

What if that key matters less than you suppose?

What if, when you pass the door, you will not be the same,
but that too is kinder than you imagine,
kind as seasons and sleep and sudden morning?

What if the poet awakens uncertain,
stiff-necked with his nose to the ground,
leaves in his beard,
thinking the soil smells of coming mushrooms,
dismissing the scent as unscientific?

What if the truest statements must remain ajar,
must linger on as questions,
stifled laughs beneath the floorboards,

or betray the natural generosity of not knowing?

Scratch Pad

- Why is grief so hungry all the time?
  And why can't it ever decide what it wants to eat?

- Humans calling themselves "outside nature" is like a child declaring themselves "a runaway" from a tent in the kitchen.

- Leaving my house to walk in the woods feels like missing someone deeply, then realizing they've been waiting in the next room the entire time.

- Any creative act, even if its core message is "to hell with all this," is a hopeful declaration that what we are all doing here together is a worthy endeavor.

- We must teach meaning-making as an empowering skill. We must reject the search for meaning as a haunting imperative.

- I feel confident that moss and fire are cousins.
  I also feel confident that I cannot explain why.

- Creativity is nourished by play. If it's possible to fail doing it, then it doesn't count as play.

- Cultivating gratitude is self-care.

- Anyone else ever get the odd feeling they are missing someone they haven't met yet? Like nostalgia aimed at an unknown future rather than an unreachable past.

Making Space

I often walk the woods alone.

Not because I crave solitude for solitude's sake,
but because when I am the only human
it is much easier to notice

other kinds of companionship.

Fifth Grade

I wish I could tell 10-year-old me that you're doing it all wrong
and that is correct.

That there is no way to be too good for danger. Or pain. Or sadness.

That uncertainty is not a character flaw.

That the search for meaning isn't a clock ticking down to "too late."

That numbness is more prison than shelter.

That when you mourn a fallen wren or a wind-split tree,
you're on the right track.

Unerring

However you manage to be at peace today
is correct.

It doesn't matter that the laundry is still piled
on the chair.

That dragon will keep your victory safe for you
until you claim it.

What matters is that you found peace today.

Memory is as fickle as fire and burns as it warms,
but risk its services anyway.

Ask it to show you a day when you did not find peace,
and by its flickering light,

see the shape of your present triumph.

Do not pester that triumph with petty questions
about petty details.

However you manage to be at peace today
is correct.

Is more than correct.

Is spectacular.

Mourning Tree

I once heard the Osage-orange called,
"The tree that mourns the mammoth."
A widowed species lost in memory.

The knobby, green fruit,
meant for eating, for seed distribution,
rots in the sun like cut lilies on a grave.

Ecosystems do not mourn with words.
They mourn with bone and bough.
Extinction is an empty place at the table.

The mammoth is not coming to dinner,
but humans, squirrels and bobwhite try to fill in,
cultivating new generations of trees.

Saplings wake in a time of absent friends,
and in ten Septembers' growth,
drop fruit 10,000 years out of season.

Sun Song

Once,
A little girl heard cicadas for the first time.
She asked, "is that the sound the sun makes?"

And, of course, the answer is, "no."
And, of course, the answer is, "yes."

The sun speaks many languages.

Come Home

When in doubt,
come home to you.
To now.
Become an acolyte of what's within reach.
Of forgiveness.
Of your desk drawer.
Of feeling each breath.
There will always be problems too big for you.
An unknown future.
A tragic world.
That's ok.
Just be you.
You're the world too.
Refocus.
Come home.

About the Author

Jarod K. Anderson has three best-selling collections of nature poetry, *Field Guide to the Haunted Forest*, *Love Notes from the Hollow Tree*, and *Leaf Litter*. His memoir *Something in the Woods Loves You* (Timber Press/Hachette 2024) explores his lifelong struggle with depression through a lens of love and gratitude for the natural world. Jarod created and voices The CryptoNaturalist podcast, a scripted show about real adoration for fictional wildlife. He lives in Ohio between a park and a cemetery.

Author Website:
www.jarodkanderson.com

The CryptoNaturalist:
Available anywhere you find podcasts or stream directly from our
website, www.cryptonaturalist.com.

To support Jarod's work and gain access to exclusive content, visit
Patreon.com/CryptoNaturalist

X: @CryptoNature
Facebook: /CryptoNaturalist
Instagram: @CryptoNaturalist